# Lots c

Written by
Elizabeth Dale

SMITHY BRIDGE
PRIMARY SCHOOL

Ransom

I am a fan.

Our team will score lots of goals.

I am the manager.
Our team will score lots of goals.

I am a forward.
I will score lots of goals.

I am a sub.
I will score lots of goals.

I am a defender.
I will score lots of goals.

I am a goalkeeper.
I will **STOP** lots of goals.

I am a defender.
I will stop lots of goals, too.

We are a team.
We will score lots of goals.

We are a team.
We will win the game.